D1258576

BARCLAY RUBINCAM
1920 - 1978

The Open Drawer, 1954

BARCLAY RUBINCAM CLOSE UP

Reminiscences by Caroline Rubincam

An Exhibition
January 27 - March 10, 1996
Brandywine River Museum
Chadds Ford, Pennsylvania

This exhibition and publication have been made possible through the generosity of Gerry Lenfest.

Cover
Memorial Day, *1951*
Oil on gesso panel, 30 1/2 × 48"
(77.5 × 121.9 cm)
Signed lower right,
    "Barclay Rubincam 1951"
Lent by Gerry Lenfest

Frontispiece
The Open Drawer, *1954*
Oil on gesso panel, 34 × 41"
(86.4 × 104.1 cm)
Signed lower right,
    "Barclay Rubincam 1954"
Lent by Gerry Lenfest

Copyright © 1995 by Brandywine Conservancy, Inc.
Library of Congress Catalog Card Number: 95-83329

Edited by Catherine E. Hutchins
Designed by Gėnė E. Harris and Glenn Weiser
Photographs for the Brandywine River Museum by Rick Echelmeyer
Printed by Pearl Pressman Liberty Communications Group

Preface

In the summer of 1986, with enthusiasm, the Brandywine River Museum purchased for its collection Barclay Rubincam's *Christmas Ball.* The painting is frequently seen in our galleries during the annual exhibition, "A Brandywine Christmas," and has become nearly a tradition in itself here. This fascinating painting also often hangs among other works in the Museum's growing and significant American still life collection and is greatly admired.

Among the many subjects Barclay Rubincam addressed, including the history and landscapes of Chester County, none inspired in him as much expressive talent as those scenes found in the present exhibition and reproduced in this publication. These are seemingly everyday objects that inspired fine work of unusual perspective with a distinctive quality to their paint surfaces. The paintings come as a wonderful surprise to many; they are not the works for which Rubincam is best known.

Rubincam is important to us for his evident artistic talent, his unique viewpoints, and because he was inspired mainly by his own origins and the sights that surrounded his home in Chester County and the Brandywine Valley. Thus, for several years we hoped to organize an exhibition celebrating the fascinating aspect of his art which combines these considerations and yet has not received as much attention as his landscapes and history paintings. This portion of his art focuses upon and endows with unusual significance such commonplace objects as chairs, tables, windows, and doors. It demonstrates Rubincam's remarkable ability to subtly invest these objects with heightened meaning.

Caroline Rubincam, the artist's widow, has contributed toward our fuller understanding of her husband's work by presenting her memories of his life and work. Her words appear on following pages and are taken from an interview she gave this curator at the Rubincam home in West Chester, Pennsylvania. The interview has been edited to remove the questions asked of her, but her responses remain. Her reminiscences evoke appealing images of the artist's life, his times and his art. Mrs. Rubincam's observations of the community in which she and her husband lived give us historical insight into people and places associated with West Chester. We are deeply grateful to her for this contribution to further appreciation of her husband's work.

The Brandywine River Museum is proud to present this carefully focused look at a singular portion of Barclay Rubincam's career. This event would not have been possible without the support of Gerry Lenfest. It was his admiration and understanding of the artist's distinctive talent which encouraged us to dedicate the Museum to this task.

Géné E. Harris
Curator of Collections

Study for Open Drawer, *c.1954*
Pencil on paper, 19 1/4 × 14 1/2"
(48.9 × 36.8 cm)
Unsigned
Lent by Mrs. Barclay Rubincam

Shadow of a Century, *1952*
Oil on gesso panel, 21 3/4 × 42"
(55.2 × 106.7 cm)
Signed lower right,
   "Barclay Rubincam 1952"
Lent anonymously

Acknowledgements

Many people deserve credit and special thanks for their assistance with this exhibition and publication. I am grateful to Mrs. Caroline Rubincam for her continuous support, especially for kindly giving much time for the interview which resulted in the principal text for this catalogue. I have benefitted from her knowledge and from her sharing invaluable information.

Everyone at the Brandywine River Museum must be very grateful to Gerry Lenfest who also has my personal thanks for his generous support and ready cooperation. He helped make the preparation of this exhibition a pleasure.

I also sincerely thank Daphne Landis and Karen Matlat for their invaluable assistance and research.

Appreciation is extended to staff members of the Brandywine River Museum for assistance and constructive advice, especially to James H. Duff, director; Jean A. Gilmore, registrar; Victoria A. Clark, assistant registrar; and Andrea Gersen, executive secretary.

Our deep gratitude goes to the generous lenders who helped make this exhibition a success: Joanne Hall Boyer, Edward and Jean E. Cotter, Karen Gordon Cunningham, Mr. and Mrs. John L. Hall, Jr., Gerry Lenfest, Museum of American Art of the Pennsylvania Academy of the Fine Arts, Mrs. Barclay Rubincam, James C. Sorber, Wilmington Trust Company and anonymous lenders.

G.E.H.

*Photograph of Barclay Rubincam
in his West Chester studio before
his painting,* **I Believe,** *1955.
Courtesy of Mrs. Barclay Rubincam*

Reminiscences by Caroline Rubincam

I guess it all started on a July morning in 1920 when Barclay was born. His parents lived in Green Valley, Pennsylvania. His mother Florence Hoopes Rubincam was of English descent, his father Jacob was of German descent. They were farmers.

Barclay's father's family had left Hesse, Germany, in the early 1800s and settled in New Jersey. His great-great-grandfather, Peter, moved the family to Green Valley in the early 1880s. Barclay was born on the old family farm on his grandfather Barclay's birthday, July 9. As a youngster he thought the Fourth of July fireworks set off at family reunions at Lenape Park were to celebrate his birthday.

He always wanted to be an artist. I remember his mother telling me that as a child he was forever picking up pencils, crayons, and brushes to draw or paint. All through school, drawing was one of his main interests, and he was excused from far too many classes in order to make posters, calendars, and stage sets. He also had a prankish streak—once he and another boy painted rabbits on the school water tower. He was in many school plays, including Gilbert & Sullivan operettas, and sometimes he didn't bother to mention this to his parents; the first they knew he was in some of those plays was when he walked out on the stage while they were in the audience.

Immediately after graduating from Unionville High School in 1939, Barclay enrolled in the Wilmington Academy of Art, which had a four-year five-day-a-week curriculum.* Part of his expenses were covered by a scholarship, most of the others he covered by taking on janitorial duties at the academy. His teachers there included Gale Hoskins and Frank Schoonover, and he studied with N. C. Wyeth in Chadds Ford.

* During World War II a dramatic decline in enrollment made it impossible for the academy to continue to operate independently. In 1943 the Wilmington Society of the Fine Arts took over the assets of the academy and classes were modified so they could be offered to the general public.

The only other place Barclay worked before becoming an artist was Warner Theater in West Chester. He was an usher in the balcony section and earned a dollar a week extra for changing the marquee. This is where I first met him. I went to see the great Charlie Chaplin in "The Great Dictator." It was May, and Barclay offered to take me home and show me his *Christmas* train, a train he'd been adding to since he was a little boy. He told me that it had a complete garden, ghosts in the cemetery, and even music. I had to go see it! He also asked me two questions: "Are you a Protestant?" and "Can you make gravy?" Soon after that we began to go out with each other. On our first date he took me to Westminster Presbyterian Church, where he had sung in the choir, and then to Valley Forge Park where we walked around. I was nineteen; he was a few weeks shy of twenty-one.

Barclay loved the Brandywine, so on another early date we went canoeing down it along with two other couples. The other two boys, Joe Entrikin and Cheston Hall were sea scouts, and the boys decided to see if they could scare the girls. Well one of them tipped the canoe too far, and we all went in. Barclay ruined a suit that wasn't paid for. And

Photograph of Caroline Hannum in 1943, before she married Barclay Rubincam. Courtesy of Mrs. Barclay Rubincam

walking up through the field afterwards, I tore my dress on a barbed wire fence. I was a sight! My mother had a fit. Oh, it was horrible.

About a year later, in June 1942, Barclay was drafted into the army. He went to Fort Gordon for basic training and was shipped overseas with the 131st engineers out of St. Louis. It so happened that late in 1942 the army was looking for somebody to paint murals for the Officers Clubs and backdrops for the USO shows that were being sent to the Pacific. Barclay had already done some sketches for soldiers to send back to their families, and when some officers looked at his record they noted that he'd been employed by Warner theater and jumped to the conclusion that he was an art student who had worked for Warner Brothers Productions in Hollywood. He was reassigned, had an apartment for the next three years, and met some very interesting celebrities. His letters home mostly mentioned how much he missed us, but sometimes he told us exactly where he was and what was going on. While Barclay was in the army, I finished college [West Chester State Teachers College] and then worked for the DuPont Company in Wilmington for fourteen months doing check reconciliation.

He was discharged November 26, 1945, and arrived home with an astounding assortment of books, maps, globes, and what have you. He set up a studio and started to paint almost immediately. We were married the following September at Valley Forge Chapel. It was a very small wedding, just the family.

After a honeymoon at Sky Top in the Poconos, we moved into an apartment on South New Street, West Chester. On August 1, 1948, we moved into a newly built house [on North New Street]. There was a sea of mud when we arrived, and the house had only the bare necessities, plus a mantel. Barclay finished the kitchen, put the chair rails in, built the bookcases—he did everything. This place was perfect, for whenever he built anything he did the cross-sections and elevations first and then made sure that during construction he had everything square and plumb. He was also very precise in positioning objects and could tell when I had touched something because it was no longer in exactly the right spot. His studio in the house was always neat.

While I concentrated on cooking and canning, Barclay did the gardening and farming. He loved the garden, and he landscaped our yard with trees and shrubs. Here too he was particular, going so far as to use chalk, string, and a yardstick even when setting out the tomatoes. (The very first year we lived in the house Barclay sent me into Yearsley's to get tomato plants. I was a town girl and had no idea of how many to buy. I came home with 125. To this day I don't know if he was too embarrassed to tell what an idiot he had for a wife, or if he thought it was part of the course.) He also transplanted trees and bushes whenever he thought they needed it or he wanted to use the spot differently. And he was a great one for cutting grass. Ofttimes while I was taking care of the children—we had four: Andre, Reginald, Ghisele, and Christopher— and getting breakfast in the mornings, he was out working in the yard and he returned to it again in the evening. As the children grew older, he taught them to weed and passed on to them his love of gardening.

Barclay never decided upon a career as an artist, he just followed his instincts. And he often wondered where his artistic ability came from, for despite the family joke that it had come from his father, there were no artists in the family. Indeed, Barclay had many artistic talents; however, this did not include literary ones. He sent me seventy-five letters during the three years he was in the army, and I don't think he wrote a letter during the nearly thirty-two years we were married. I did all his correspondence, and I paid all the bills.

Before he was drafted, Barclay had shown his paintings at the Wilmington Academy of Art and at the American Legion in Kennett Square. In the years after he returned, he was exhibiting at the Chester County Art Association and local banks and especially the Village Flower Shop owned by Henry and Robert Guss in West Chester.

I had known the Guss family since childhood, for Bob had been a teen-age lifeguard at Lenape when I was a youngster. In the 1950s and 1960s Bob's flower shop did a great deal of business. Many times Barclay would drop off a painting in the morning, and in the afternoon one of the bankers or lawyers who had passed by on the way to lunch would stop on the way back with a check. Barclay sold an awful lot of paintings through that shop.

Photograph of Rubincam in the Army, New Caledonia, South Pacific, 1942-1945. Courtesy of Mrs. Barclay Rubincam

Barclay donated his time and his works to the community, including the United Fund of Greater West Chester, the 175th Anniversary of West Chester in 1974, the West Chester Chamber of Commerce, Upland Country Day School scholarship fund, the Chester County Association for Retarded Citizens, and the Chester County Art Association. He also belonged to several organizations, including Chester County Historical Society, Chester County Art Association, Wilmington Society of the Fine Arts, Church of the Holy Trinity, and for a while to the Philadelphia Art Alliance. But to tell the truth, he wasn't great on going to meetings.

He also did not like being asked to judge paintings our friends had purchased. If they stopped by and asked, "Barclay, we got this on our vacation—what do you think of it?" he always replied: "Well you like it. You bought it didn't you?" But he was more than happy to oblige friends who were building a new house and called to ask "Barclay, how about coming up for dinner? And could you bring your sketch pad; we want a mantel, and a bookcase too."

Throughout his life, Barclay's work habits were very regular, but the hours he kept were hideous. He began painting right after breakfast, and following a break for lunch, he painted or sketched in the afternoon. If working at home, he painted while listening to classical music. (He had a fantastic collection of records and for a while he loved to paint to Wagner.) Late in the afternoon he rested or went to meet the school bus or train bringing the children home. In the evenings when he was not giving art classes (in his studio or in other people's houses in West Chester or in a recreational center in Kennett Square), he'd go out to his garage and construct a frame—he made all of his frames. He also did a lot of cleaning of paintings—not so much toward the end but in the beginning—and quite a bit of restoration. And he did the work in the yard on top of all of this. I couldn't keep up with him.

Barclay's wonderful memory and great sense of humor served him well because he loved to talk and visit. Having been raised on a farm, he was especially interested in the nostalgic agrarian society, and on his many visits to Longwood Gardens he'd often meet with old friends and

Photograph of Rubincam's studio on North New Street, West Chester, 1948. Courtesy of Mrs. Barclay Rubincam

reminisce. He also met lots of people when he was working on his snow scenes, all of which he did on site. (He liked the winter, and his winter scenes came up very well in pastel.) Usually, if he didn't know the landowners personally, he would call in advance to let them know that he was going to be doing a painting on their property, and a good many of the owners made a point of coming out to talk with him, which meant he met lots of interesting people and heard lots of new tales. Other people simply stopped by the studio on a regular basis, especially on bank holidays. Many of them confessed to being discontent but claimed they couldn't change careers because they had mortgages to pay and children to feed, clothe, and educate. Barclay's standard response was "You pay the price for the way you want to live." He often added: "You have a steady paycheck and I don't." It amazed him that so many people were willing to settle for second best. Painting is all he ever wanted to do—no other profession entered his mind.

One of Barclay's great friends was Chris Sanderson who had a life-long passion for local history. Chris was a character. Barclay and I had visited his museum as children, and Barclay did Chris's portrait in late 1940s (Sanderson Museum). Once we invited him to dinner. I prepared roast beef, mashed potatoes, apple pie, and probably a vegetable. Well, Chris wouldn't stay—the meal was too fancy. Shortly after that, I landed in Chester County Hospital. Down the hall was Chris Sanderson, hospitalized for malnutrition. Well, Barclay went to see him and discovered that Chris even had a guest book in his room. The local newspaper reported that nobody received more mail or had more people calling him than Chris. When Chris left, it took seven people to carry his things out of the hospital. What a riot.

Every year Chris came to the Easter Sunday services at Church of the Holy Trinity but could only stay for the processional because he had to get to WCOJ, his radio station. But he always came. When he died the church was packed. Members of the West Chester High School band marched up the street playing "Battle Hymn of the Republic." He was greatly loved.

Barclay was fascinated with local history. A large number of his paintings deal with the history of Chester County, especially the history of West Chester, and included sites and buildings with which he was familiar. Among his major historical works is *The Trap Is Sprung* (1971), in which he depicted British troops crossing Brandywine Creek in September 1777 as Quaker farmers look on. In another, *The Battle of West Chester* (1970), he showed the Uplanders coming to West Chester. In *The Hospital at Yellow Springs* (1975) he featured the only Revolutionary War hospital commissioned by the Continental Congress. His *Hessian Soldiers Leaving the Unicorn Inn, September 11, 1777* (1973) is another in that Battle of the Brandywine series. Barclay also did pastels that focused on the nineteenth century. Two of them show different aspects of the same corner: *West Chester, c. 1840, Winter: Northwest of North High Street, Across the Porch of the Turk's Head Inn to the Early Courthouse,* and *West Chester, c. 1840, Winter: Northwest View from Market Street to the Turk's Head Inn* (both 1974). Another work commemorating Lafayette's triumphant return to America in 1824-1825 is *Lafayette Passing Strodes Mill* (1966).

When he and I talked about his art he loved to explain what he was doing and why he was painting it. He was always open to new topics, and whenever he heard something on the radio or television that was interesting, he invariably sent me to the library to find out more about it. Over the years I did a tremendous amount of his research, and Dorothy Lapp at the historical society was most generous with her assistance. When he was planning a painting of a historical event I often brought home books for him to study. If his painting was to deal with more recent events, he often interviewed people. For example, before he did his painting of the yellow trolley car, he visited with a motorman who had driven a similar one; he needed to know the details about how a trolley operated. And of course, he always enjoyed people telling him stories about what had happened in bygone years.

He did historical maps of West Chester, the Battle of the Brandywine, Valley Forge, and Gettysburg. These were elaborate and based on considerable research. The one of West Chester depicts the old parts of town and the prominent people—it shows how West Chester used to look. The map of Gettysburg took a lot of work. He practically lived out there one whole summer. In 1953 he finished the second phase

*Rubincam's West Chester studio, showing the painting, **Green Valley School House,** 1977. Courtesy of Mrs. Barclay Rubincam*

of it, and that took several trips more. I couldn't go because I had morning sickness; my second child, Reginald, was on the way.

Although Barclay did some paintings on commission, most of the time he simply painted and hoped to find a market when he was done. He usually had a pastel and an oil going at the same time. He often worked with sketches that were piecemeal, then he would do the pastel and the oil in a sort of progression—the pastel was very often the complete work from a sketch. He usually hung the completed painting on the wall to study it before he declared it "finished." Often during that stage he would ask me if it needed more color here or a detail added there. When he was satisfied, he went in search of a buyer. He could always remember who had expressed a desire for a scene that had a specific element, such as a covered bridge, and he'd call that person, deliver the painting, hang it, and say "Look at it for a while, then if you want it, fine. If you don't want it, somebody else will." Ultimately what Barclay was particularly pleased about was that people bought his paintings for their homes and gave them a place of honor. They didn't consider his work an investment; they considered it a cherished possession. They might only be able to afford this one painting, but they knew they were getting a very special painting. That made him feel good.

Since Barclay always painted on site, the children and I—plus many a peanut-butter sandwich—often accompanied him during the summer. He loved to paint the Brandywine and the life along it, such as skinny dipping near the covered bridge [*Boys along the Brandywine,* 1969] and ice skating [*Skating on the Brandywine,* ca. 1963], and when he needed to put people in his paintings he very often included himself, one of our children, or one of our pets. One of the very few non-family members to pose for Barclay was Dr. Slagle, our next door neighbor, who was an English professor and an Episcopal priest. He posed for *Sentry at Birmingham,* wearing a hat that had belonged to a member of the Delaware militia and carrying a rifle, both of which had been lent by Frank Schoonover.

Barclay's portraits were almost always commissioned. The ones that were most intriguing were the sixty-year-old sitters who wanted to look twenty. Another one that I recall was a period piece—a young girl holding a bible with flowers in her lap—that is very much a character portrait. Barclay captured her innocence. Barclay painted a portrait of our son Andre in 1954. Kennett Square Lions Club commissioned him to do Monroe L. Nute, president of the International Lions in 1958. The following year Barclay painted William Burgess, president of Southeast National Bank (present-day Fidelity Bank), and William Brosius, president of the National Bank of Chester County.

The paintings in this exhibition hold an assortment of memories for me.

Generations (1950) is an early painting. Barclay included both a young tree and an enduring house. And the house has character: its very visible cracks hint at the amount of living that has gone on in the house.

Morning Glory (1950) features the vine that used to be at the front door. He later moved it because we didn't want the bell to be appropriated by the vine. The bell had long stood in his parents' yard and had been rung by friends and family members as they serenaded his parents when they returned from their honeymoon.

It's Raining (1951) shows the barn on the Route 52 property where Barclay's family lived when he was in high school. Barclay could look out his bedroom window and see the rain on the barn, and whether or not to put on his all-weather clothes. Barclay loved painting knotted and gnarled trees.The paintings in this exhibition hold an assortment of memories for me.

Memorial Day (1951) is a composite picture. The setting is the porch of his parents' Lenape Road home. Family members used to sit on the porch swing and spit watermelon seeds into the yard. The chair is one Barclay bought for me at Gilbertsville when I was nursing our first baby, André. The lawn mower was ours.

Tomatoes on Windowsill (1952) is another composite scene. The tomatoes are ones Barclay grew in his garden. The setting is Birmingham Meeting House.

In his art Barclay had a wonderful ability to magnify and intensify ordinary objects in a rather unusual way, and bring objects close up. It was an innate talent. And many of the items in Barclay's paintings were ours, a goodly number of which were heirlooms. The corner cupboard in *Shadow of a Century* (1952) (p.8) is one of the few pieces of furniture we bought. The Tucker pitcher in that painting came from my father's family. For *The Open Drawer* (1954) (frontispiece) he used a chest that also came from my father's family, and the top drawer of that chest is inscribed with the names of all the owners since 1816. When he first painted this, there was no ribbon; he added that later.

Inheritance (1953) shows the painted, drop-leaf Sheraton table that had belonged to my grandparents, and then my aunt. We were given it in 1948, and have dined on it every day since then. On the table sits our Tucker pitcher, which was made in Philadelphia of clay dug from Chester County. The two silhouettes are of members of my father's family.

Christmas Ball (1954) shows an ornament from his first Christmas tree that had been given him by grandmother Hoopes. It rests on the mantel that came out of the old Farmer's Hotel and is now at the Chester County Historical Society. The sprig was added at the suggestion of Andrew Wyeth.

I Believe (1955) was inspired by Good Friday. It is a view through our living room window. The forsythia is a sign of the resurrection. The Bible belonged to Lavinia Roberts Hoopes Hannum, my great-grandmother. The image reminds me of Barclay's faith, which was very strong even though he didn't go to church as often as I wished.

Sconneltown School (1957) depicts a small portion of a one-room schoolhouse at the corner of Sconneltown Road and Birmingham Road in West Chester. It is now a private residence, but the school had a little outhouse and seesaws, and I remember riding the seesaws as a child. Barclay painted this the last year classes were held in the building.

Sentry at Birmingham (1959) depicts the sentry guarding that same meeting house and protecting the wounded soldiers hospitalized there during the 1777 Battle of the Brandywine. It is also a subtle reminder of the unknown soldiers from the Revolutionary War that are buried nearby. When working on this, Barclay had Dr. Slagle pose against the garage wall in the daytime. To make sure that he was rendering the shadows accurately, he took a lantern up to the meeting house in the early hours of the morning.

Gone for the Fourth (The Flag) was painted at Dick and Betty Matlat's house on Westtown Road in 1960. We were introduced to the Matlats at a party that Jim and Myra Sorber gave in 1951, and both couples became our life-long friends. It was Jim Sorber who built a new studio for Barclay in 1962. Dick and Betty's house had three stories, but mostly we sat and talked at the table in their huge kitchen.

Primary Election Returns (1963) is set on the Birmingham Meeting House grounds, showing a building that used to be a school. Posting the election results on the door of the polling place was a local tradition that allowed rural voters to learn who had won and lost. In a sense Barclay's painting is a record of that long-standing local tradition.

Lilacs on the Chest (1965) is a different view of the same chest of drawers in *The Open Drawer.* The lilacs were some of the many that used to grow in our yard. They were a gift from our Warrington cousins.

Sandy Flash (1974) was inspired by James Fitzgerald (alias Sandy Flash), who spied for both the Continental and the British armies and was hanged in Chester. Barclay relied on Bayard Taylor's description of Fitzgerald in *The Story of Kennett.* Because Fitzgerald was a blacksmith Barclay set the painting in front of a closed smithy and placed an anvil to one side. The ghost of Sandy Flash reportedly rides up and down Route 52 carrying messages, and years ago Chris Sanderson performed the role of "Sandy Flash" in plays that the Brandywiners staged at Longwood Gardens.

Class Room Memories (1976) shows elements of a typical classroom when Barclay and I were children, a time in which children saluted the flag everyday. The picture on the wall is one of Gilbert Stuart's paintings of Washington. Barclay designed this painting to evoke memories of a bygone era. He had not gone to a one-room schoolhouse, but his father had. Barclay also painted another picture with a related theme. It shows a boy coming up to the old school (*Green Valley School House,* 1977). The boy represents Barclay's father; the building used to be a ladies school.

Barclay borrowed the horse for *Rocking Horse* (1960) from a Chadds Ford antiques dealer and set it in Matlat's attic on Westtown Road. He said that it reminded him of his childhood and his father's farmhouse attic. The walnuts scattered over floorboards came from our front yard.

Barclay loved trains all his life, and spent considerable time working on his trains each Christmas. In 1977, he made a huge plaster-of-paris tunnel and used 400 feet of wiring. The night before he went to the hospital for his operation, he stayed up way past 2 a.m. putting the finishing touches on it because he was afraid that afterwards he wouldn't be able to work on his train. It simply had to be done for Christmas. Our children, as had Barclay since his own childhood, loved the train. Every year Santa Claus brought something new for it. This particular year our youngest, Christopher, had seen a new train at a local store and told Barclay he wanted it. Barclay bought it and hid it. Christmas morning came, and there was no train among his presents. Barclay took Chris upstairs to play with the train while I did the breakfast dishes and had Chris push the switch. Out came the new train.

Much of the time Barclay was in Chester County Hospital his mind focused on music, so we often turned the radio on. At one point he refused to let a nurse give him a shot because he was listening to "Faust." His mind was back and forth. When they transferred him to the Veterans Hospital in Elsmere, Delaware, the driver wondered aloud which turn to take as they neared Wilmington and Barclay, in a moment of lucidity, told him. Days later, Barclay asked me if I'd remembered to put the sleigh bells on the Christmas tree. He could be terribly confused. I was there the day he died of cancer on 24th of June 1978.

Even during his illness he did not stop drawing. Many nurses came in and made a big fuss over him. One girl said "Mr. Rubincam will you draw a picture on my apron," and before the day was out her whole graduating class had come in—he was drawing to the very end.

[Rubincam's paintings were exhibited at the Pennsylvania Academy of the Fine Arts, Philadelphia Art Alliance, Wilmington Society of the Fine Arts, Hagley Museum, Toledo Museum of Art, West Chester State Teachers College (now West Chester State University), Pennsylvania State University, Brandywine River Museum, Brecks Mill in Wilmington, and Yellow Springs Historical Society. The Tatnall School in Wilmington, Fidelity Bank, Chester County Historical Society, Wilmington Trust, Pennsylvania Academy of the Fine Arts, Commonwealth Federal Savings and Loan, and Chester County Hospital are among the institutions owning his paintings. Private owners of Barclay's works live throughout the West Chester-Kennett Square-Unionville area; others live as close as Washington, D.C., and as far away as Illinois, Montana, Oregon, and Washington.]

Catalogue of the Exhibition

Morning Glory, 1950
Oil on gesso panel, 33 × 39 3/4"
(83.8 × 39.7 cm)
Signed lower right
  "Barclay Rubincam 1950"
Lent by Joanne Hall Boyer

It's Raining, *1951*
Oil on gesso panel, 41 × 34"
(104.1 × 86.4 cm)
Signed lower right,
   "Barclay Rubincam 1951"
Lent by Gerry Lenfest

Generations, 1950
Oil on gesso panel, 36 × 48"
(91.4 × 121.9 cm)
Signed lower right,
*   "Barclay Rubincam 1950"*
Lent by James C. Sorber

Tomatoes on Windowsill, *1952*
Oil on gesso panel, 24 × 45"
(60.9 × 114.3 cm)
Signed lower right,
   "Barclay Rubincam 1952"
Wilmington Trust Company

Study for Inheritance, *c. 1953*
Charcoal on paper, 19 × 24 3/4"
(48.3 × 62.9 cm)
Unsigned
Lent by Mrs. Barclay Rubincam

Inheritance, 1953
Oil on gesso panel, 24 × 48"
(60.9 × 121.9 cm)
Signed lower right,
    "Barclay Rubincam 1953"
Lent by Joanne Hall Boyer

Christmas Ball, *1954*
Oil on gesso panel, 24 × 40"
(61 × 101.6 cm)
Signed lower right,
    "Barclay Rubincam 1954"
Collection of the
Brandywine River Museum,
Museum purchase

I Believe, 1955
Oil on gessoed masonite panel,
19 15/16 × 39 15/16"
(50.8 × 101.4 cm)
Signed lower right,
    "Barclay Rubincam 1955"
Lent by Museum of American Art of the
Pennsylvania Academy of the Fine Arts,
Philadelphia, John Lambert Fund

Rocking Horse, 1960
Pastel on paper, 28 × 38"
(71.1 × 96.5 cm)
Signed lower right,
    "Barclay Rubincam 1960"
Lent anonymously

Sconneltown School, *1957*
Pastel on paper, 24 × 38"
(60.9 × 96.5 cm)
Signed lower right,
   "Barclay Rubincam 1957"
Lent by Mr. and Mrs. John L. Hall, Jr.

Study for Sentry at Birmingham, *1959*
Oil on board, 16 3/4 × 19 1/2"
(42.5 × 49.5 cm)
Signed lower right,
   "Barclay Rubincam 1959"
Lent by James C. Sorber

Sentry at Birmingham, 1959
Oil on gesso panel, 38 1/2 × 49 3/4"
(97.8 × 126.4 cm)
Signed lower right,
  "Barclay Rubincam 1959"
Lent by James C. Sorber

Gone for the Fourth (The Flag), 1960
Oil on gesso panel, 40 × 20"
(101.6 × 50.8 cm)
Signed lower right,
  "Barclay Rubincam 1960"
Lent anonymously

Primary Election Returns, 1963
Oil on gesso panel, 48 × 24 1/4"
(122 × 61.5 cm)
Signed lower right,
  "Barclay Rubincam 1963"
Lent by Karen Gordon Cunningham

Lilacs on the Chest, *1965*
Pastel on paper, 23 1/2 × 38 1/2"
(59.7 × 97.8 cm)
Signed lower right,
  "Barclay Rubincam -65-"
Lent by Edward and Jean E. Cotter

Sandy Flash, 1974
Oil on gesso panel, 24 × 48"
(60.9 × 121.9 cm)
Signed lower right,
    "Barclay Rubincam -74-"
Lent anonymously

Class Room Memories, *1976*
Oil on gesso panel, 21 1/2 × 37 1/2"
(54.6 × 95.2 cm)
Signed lower right,
    "Barclay Rubincam 1976"
Lent anonymously